READING POWER

Women Who Shaped History

Coretta Scott King
Civil Rights Activist

Joanne Mattern

The Rosen Publishing Group's
PowerKids Press™
New York

Published in 2003 by The Rosen Publishing Group, Inc.
29 East 21st Street, New York, NY 10010

Copyright © 2003 by The Rosen Publishing Group, Inc.

All rights reserved. No part of this book may be reproduced in any form without permission in writing from the publisher, except by a reviewer.

First Edition

Book Design: Erica Clendening

Photo Credits: Cover, p. 5 © Vernon Merritt III/TimePix; p. 4 American Missionary Association Archives Addendum, Amistad Research Center at Tulane University; pp. 6–7 Library of Congress, Prints and Photographs Division; p. 7 courtesy the New England Conservatory of Music; p. 9 © Donald Uhrbrock/TimePix; p. 10 © Corbis; pp. 11, 14 © Flip Schulke/Corbis; pp. 12–13 © Sam Melhorn, The Commercial Appeal; p. 13 © Bob Fitch/BlackStar/TimePix; p. 15 © Andrew Hudson; p. 17 © Hulton/Archive/Getty Images; p. 18 © David & Peter Turnley/Corbis; p. 19 © AP/Wide World Photos; p. 20 © Bettmann/Corbis; p. 21 © Diana Walker/TimePix

Library of Congress Cataloging-in-Publication Data

Mattern, Joanne, 1963-
  Coretta Scott King : civil rights activist / Joanne Mattern.
    v. cm. — (Women who shaped history)
  Includes bibliographical references and index.
  Contents: In the beginning — The Civil Rights Movement — Continuing the cause — Working for world peace.
  ISBN 0-8239-6504-X (lib. bdg.)
  1. King, Coretta Scott, 1927—Juvenile literature. 2. African American women—Biography—Juvenile literature. 3. African Americans—Biography—Juvenile literature. 4. Civil rights workers—United States—Biography—Juvenile literature. 5. King, Martin Luther, Jr., 1929-1968—Juvenile literature. 6. African Americans—Civil rights—History—20th century—Juvenile literature. 7. Civil rights movements—United States—History—20th century—Juvenile literature. [1. King, Coretta Scott, 1927- 2. Civil rights workers. 3. African Americans—Biography. 4. Women—Biography. 5. King, Martin Luther, Jr., 1929-1968. 6. Civil rights movements.] I. Title.
E185.97.K47 M38 2003
323'.092—dc21

2002002931

Contents

In the Beginning	4
The Civil Rights Movement	10
Continuing the Cause	14
Working for World Peace	18
Glossary	22
Resources	23
Index/Word Count	24
Note	24

In the Beginning

Coretta Scott King has worked most of her life for peace and equal rights for everyone. She was born on April 27, 1927, in Alabama. At that time, African Americans did not have the same rights as other people. People treated the Scott family badly because they were African Americans.

Coretta Scott went to Lincoln High School in Marion, Alabama.

Coretta Scott King

Coretta Scott was a very good student. She was also a good singer. In 1945, she went to college in Ohio.

Coretta Scott studied teaching and music while at Antioch College in Ohio.

After college, Coretta Scott went to Boston, Massachusetts, to study music. There, she met another student named Martin Luther King, Jr.

Coretta Scott attended school in Boston, Massachusetts, to study music.

7

On June 18, 1953, Coretta Scott and Martin Luther King, Jr. were married. They moved to Montgomery, Alabama. There, Martin Luther King, Jr. worked as a pastor in a church. The Kings had four children: Yolanda; Martin Luther, III; Dexter; and Bernice.

The King family was very close. Pictured here in a photo taken in 1960 are: (from left) Martin Luther King, III; Martin Luther King, Jr.; Yolanda King; and Coretta Scott King. Bernice and Dexter King were not born yet.

The Civil Rights Movement

The Kings worked hard for civil rights. They wanted all people to be treated equally. They gave speeches to tell people why racism should be against the law. Coretta Scott King also sang in concerts to raise money for their nonviolent movement for civil rights.

Coretta Scott King has given many speeches against racism.

The Kings' work often put them in danger. In 1956, their home was bombed by people who wanted to stop the Kings' work. No one was hurt and the Kings continued their struggle for equal rights for all.

> The Kings (front row) walked in marches around the country to show that they wanted equal rights for everyone.

On April 4, 1968, Martin Luther King, Jr. was shot and killed in Memphis, Tennessee.

> Just four days after Martin Luther King, Jr. died, Coretta Scott King (center) led 50,000 people in a march in Memphis to honor him.

Coretta Scott King was very sad, but she did not stop working for civil rights.

Even though Coretta Scott King was very sad after her husband died, she kept working for equal rights for all.

13

Continuing the Cause

In 1968, Coretta Scott King started the King Center in Atlanta, Georgia, to honor her husband. She became the Center's first president. The King Center works for equal rights and peace for all people.

Martin Luther King, Jr.

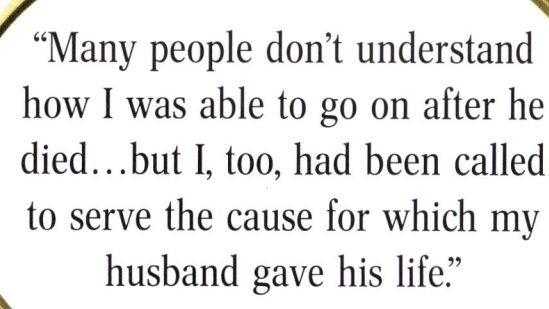

"Many people don't understand how I was able to go on after he died…but I, too, had been called to serve the cause for which my husband gave his life."
—Coretta Scott King

The King Center was started to remember Martin Luther King, Jr. and to continue his work.

Coretta Scott King also writes about her work. In 1969, she wrote a book about her life with Martin Luther King, Jr. She did not want people to forget what he had worked for and believed. She has also written for newspapers and magazines.

Now You Know

The Coretta Scott King Award is given each year to an African American who has written or illustrated an outstanding children's book.

Coretta Scott King wrote her book, *My Life with Martin Luther King, Jr.*, in 1969.

Working for World Peace

Coretta Scott King has worked hard for peace around the world. She has worked with groups and leaders of many different countries, such as Greece and South Africa. She has won many awards for her work.

- Coretta Scott King has worked with many world leaders, including Nelson Mandela (left) from South Africa.

"Those of you who believe in what Martin Luther King, Jr. stood for, I would challenge you today to see that his spirit never dies."
—Coretta Scott King

Coretta Scott King has received awards for her work from more than 40 colleges.

In 1995, Coretta Scott King turned over the job of running the King Center to her son, Dexter King. Today, she still speaks and writes about civil rights. She has started and helped many groups to carry on her work. Coretta Scott King has worked her entire life to make the world a better place to live.

Time Line

April 27, 1927 *Coretta Scott is born in Alabama*

1945 *Goes to college in Ohio*

1951 *Goes to school in Boston and meets Martin Luther King, Jr.*

1953 *Marries Martin Luther King, Jr.*

April 4, 1968 *Martin Luther King, Jr. is killed in Memphis, Tennessee*

Now You Know

In 1983, Martin Luther King, Jr.'s birthday was made a national holiday. Coretta Scott King worked hard to make this happen. Today, more than 100 countries honor Martin Luther King, Jr. in special ways.

- President Ronald Reagan (sitting) signed the law making Martin Luther King, Jr. Day a national holiday. Standing behind him are (left to right) Christine Ferris, Martin Luther King, Jr.'s sister; Dexter King; and Coretta Scott King.

1969 Writes My Life with Martin Luther King, Jr.

1995 Son, Dexter King, starts running the King Center

1968 Leads a march in honor of Martin Luther King, Jr.; starts the King Center

1983 Martin Luther King, Jr. Day is made a national holiday

Glossary

bombed (**bahmd**) to have blown up something

cause (**kawz**) an idea or goal that many people care about

civil (**sihv**-uhl) having to do with people's private rights

Civil Rights Movement (**sihv**-uhl **ryts moov**-muhnt) events that took place during the 1950s and 1960s that worked toward getting equal rights for all people

college (**kahl**-ihj) a school where you can study after high school

concerts (**kahn**-suhrts) music shows

illustrated (**ihl**-uh-stray-tuhd) to have drawn pictures

nonviolent (nahn-**vy**-uh-luhnt) peaceful; without causing harm

pastor (**pas**-tuhr) the person who is in charge of a church

racism (**ray**-sihz-uhm) judging people based on how they look or the color of their skin

rights (**ryts**) things that a person is allowed to do

Resources

Books

Coretta Scott King
by Cynthia Fitterer Klingel
Child's World (1999)

Dare to Dream: Coretta Scott King and the Civil Rights Movement
by Angela Shelf Medearis
Puffin Books (1999)

Web Sites

Due to the changing nature of Internet links, PowerKids Press has developed an online list of Web sites related to the subjects of this book. This site is updated regularly. Please use this link to access the list:

http://www.powerkidslinks.com/wsh/crsk/

Index

B
bombed, 11

C
civil rights, 10, 13, 20
college, 6–7, 19–20
concerts, 10

K
King Center, 14–15,
   20–21

P
pastor, 8

R
racism, 10
rights, 4, 11, 13–14

Word Count: 474
Note to Librarians, Teachers, and Parents
   If reading is a challenge, Reading Power is a solution! Reading Power is perfect for readers who want high-interest subject matter at an accessible reading level. These fact-filled, photo-illustrated books are designed for readers who want straightforward vocabulary, engaging topics, and a manageable reading experience. With clear picture/text correspondence, leveled Reading Power books put the reader in charge. Now readers have the power to get the information they want and the skills they need in a user-friendly format.